Business-Driven Digital Product Design

Graphic Design in Brand Storytelling

by Fireart Studio

*"The artist sees the world as it is.
The artist tells a story that resonates."*
- Seth Godin, Marketing Consultant, Author

Authors

Dima Venglinski, Founder & CEO of Fireart Studio
Tolik Nguen, Art Director at Fireart Studio
Valeria Rimkevich, Art Director at Fireart Studio
Dmitrij Hladkyi, Art Director at Fireart Studio
Dana Kachan, Editor

Copyright © 2019 by Fireart Studio.

All rights reserved. No part of this publication may be uploaded or posted online without the prior written permission of the publisher.

For permission requests, write to the publisher, addressed "Attention: Permissions Request," to client@fireart.studio.

Business-Driven Digital Product Design:
Graphic Design In Brand Storytelling

Contents

Introduction

Chapter I. The Art of Digital Illustration for Business

Digital Illustration Helps Connect Brands With Their Customers
5 Ways to Amplify User Interfaces With Digital Illustration
Digital Drawing: The How-To Guide on Using Tools for Creativity
Case Study: How We Created The Collection of Digital Illustrations for Google

Chapter II. Digital Art Goes Live: Explain Business Ideas Creatively With Animation

How Can Animation Empower Marketing?
8 Creative Uses of The Animation to Increase CTR and Sales
Lifting The Veil To Our Animation Production Process
Case Study: How We Produced an Explainer Video for Swiss Fin Lab

Conclusion

Business-Driven Digital Product Design:
Graphic Design In Brand Storytelling

Introduction

In the fast-paced world, business approaches and marketing tactics are changing all the time. However, some old-school marketing practices still work even today. We are visual creatures, and we often love brands with eyes.

In spite of the laws of logic, customers commonly prefer brands that offer them an emotional and aesthetic appeal. The quality of products or services provided by a company plays a huge role. However, a visual online presence is critical for business success too.

The businesses that invest in their visual styles will surely take advantage. The eye-catching graphic design elements incorporated in user interfaces, brand identity, or advertising, help a brand to express its unique personality and engage customers.

The visual constituent matters. Business graphic designers are more than visual translators of the brand's concepts. They can significantly contribute to the company's success by crafting digital illustrations and animated videos that will capture the audience's attention, sell products and services, and open new markets.

These design elements are typically playful graphics that can help your business appear friendly and communicate a message more organically. Both digital illustration and animation can persuade, inform, and influence your customers. They can enhance your brand messaging and help your business express emotions.

Fireart Studio takes pride in providing graphic design services for global brands, such as Google, Pipedrive, Atlassian, Codio, and plenty of others. We have helped these giants to amplify their opportunities and build an even stronger brand image with graphic design solutions and would like to share our experience with you.

In this book, you can learn about the creative uses of modern digital illustration and animation for business. Here you can discover how a brand can benefit from graphic design and use it to set better communication with its customers. We hope our team's insights will help you design a more robust online business image, connect with your audience, and increase sales.

Are you ready for a big graphic design adventure that will help you see the brand's visual presence in the new light? Keep on reading!

Business-Driven Digital Product Design:
Graphic Design In Brand Storytelling

Chapter I.

The Art of Digital Illustration for Business

Illustration by Andy Selimov

Digital Illustration Helps Connect Brands With Their Customers

"Organize the talented. Connect the disconnected."
Seth Godin, Marketing Consultant, Author

Illustration by Julia Hanke

Today's business is not about how to sell a product only, but how to sell an emotion related to it. Forward-thinking entrepreneurs are not interested in one-time conversions anymore but strive to generate returning customers. To build long-term relationships with a target audience, brands should interact with an audience on a more emotional level. Digital illustration on a user interface, printed item, or branded stuff is an excellent way to create an emotional appeal to customers.

Business-Driven Digital Product Design:
Graphic Design In Brand Storytelling

"A picture is worth a thousand words."

Ben Shneiderman, computer scientist

Evoking positive emotions associated with a brand, it can become the key to your target users' hearts. In this chapter, we will outline the incredible applications of digital illustration and the ways how it can bring even more value to the business.

Why Does a Business Need Artistic Illustrations?

An illustration builds emotional bonds with a target audience

"What people want is the extra, the emotional bonus they get when they buy something they love."

Seth Godin, Marketing Consultant, Author

Illustration by Dmitry Kazak

Business-Driven Digital Product Design:
Graphic Design In Brand Storytelling

People are often driven by emotions. It is neither good nor bad, but just a fact. Smart entrepreneurs and marketers should consider it when creating an online business presence.

Using a digital illustration on a website or mobile application, you get more chances to distinguish your business in a crowded sea of alternatives. An illustration incorporated in the overall visual design helps provide a "wow" effect when a user enters a site or app. It motivates people to opt for this brand because it offers them pleasure, which is a reward in and of itself.

Digital illustration based on interesting metaphors can convey the brand's values and messages

> *"Illustration provides a great opportunity to communicate because it abstracts an idea."*
>
> **Steve Peck**, Creative Director
> working for Apple, Dropbox, and Samsung

Illustration by Lera Kuntsevich

You might have heard many times that we are visual creatures. According to Freeze, it is estimated that visual perception is 80% memory and 20% input through the eyes.

Business-Driven Digital Product Design:
Graphic Design In Brand Storytelling

Just look at this lovely illustration for a website of a dog beauty salon created by Lera Kuntseva for Fireart. This image perfectly communicates the brand's values through plenty of cute details. It says that this salon is a place where everybody will do everything possible to turn your pet's life into paradise.

An illustration is a creative way to tell the brand's story and demonstrate product features

"Design is an opportunity to continue telling the story, not just to sum everything up."

Tate Linden, President & Chief Creative Officer at Stokefire

We couldn't help but agree with Tate Linden. The design with narrative illustrations can tell a story in an even more engaging way. Digital illustrations are often used by brands to accompany marketing messages, demonstrate product features, or tell the company's history.

Illustration by Dmitrij and Mari Seroshtanova

Business-Driven Digital Product Design:
Graphic Design In Brand Storytelling

For example, in this beautiful illustration created by Dmitrij and Mari Seroshtanova for Fireart Studio, you can see the features of a volumetric camera depicted in a set of creative illustrations on a website. They not only help convey the information about the product's characteristics but also emphasize the brand's style.

The search results on Google are saturated with websites selling similar products. Although, those companies that have invested in a beautiful visual style (and in engaging illustrations, in particular), will surely win this battle.

An eloquent digital illustration helps transfer a marketing message

> *"Illustration allows you to exaggerate your expression in effective ways and provides room for interpretation and imagination, which can make your message more powerful."*

Steve Peck, Creative Director working for Apple, Dropbox, and Samsung

Illustration by Dmitrij Hladkyi

There are hundreds of sparkling drinks in stores. Which one to choose, what brand to prefer? We subconsciously want products of those brands, which we have previously heard about

Business-Driven Digital Product Design:
Graphic Design In Brand Storytelling

online. This illustration, created by Dmitrij Hladkyi for Fireart Studio, conveys a marketing message "The Best Drinks In The Galaxy," used in advertising by our client, a sparkling drink brand. This illustration perfectly complements a marketing message.

To stand out on the web today has become even more challenging than ever. Many brands use engaging illustrations to grab the audience's attention by creative advertising. The brand identity elements used in ads can greatly work for brand awareness. However, the audience's interest can be quickly exhausted if they use only them.

Good advertising continually needs to be fueled by creativity to perform well. An eye-catching illustration will add freshness and emotions to your ads. It considerably raises chances to be noticed by a target audience. People will not quickly scroll your ad if there is a fun character or humorous visual metaphor. On the contrary, they would like to know what a brand stands behind this ad.

Eliminate negative user experience using lovely illustrations

"If you want to find a bug you must think like a bug... You must behave like a bug... You must be a bug."

The Unknown

11

Illustration by Lily

When creating a product, QA engineers and developers always try to find out and eliminate all the bugs and technical issues possible. User testing is the key to a smooth and intuitive user experience.

"It is almost impossible to develop a perfect product from the first attempt. The product is made not only by people but also by a dynamic improvement process. Designers and developers should provide micro-transformations at different stages of a development cycle. They must check whether each interaction is well-done, and all features function properly."

Dima Venglinski, Founder & CEO of Fireart Studio

tweet this

In spite of efforts spent to avoid bags, user experiences may still be imperfect. It depends on the human factor.

"To err is human... But what if to use this "error" to build more "human" and warm relationships between a brand and users? You can display an amusing character to mobile app users as an

Business-Driven Digital Product Design:
Graphic Design In Brand Storytelling

excuse for a technical issue. It may help you not only eliminate the negative user experience but also raise the user's mood, increase his loyalty, and make an app even more lovable. To err is not so bad if you do it like an artist."

Tolik Nguen, Art Director at Fireart Studio

Use onboarding illustrations to greet, engage, and inform mobile app users

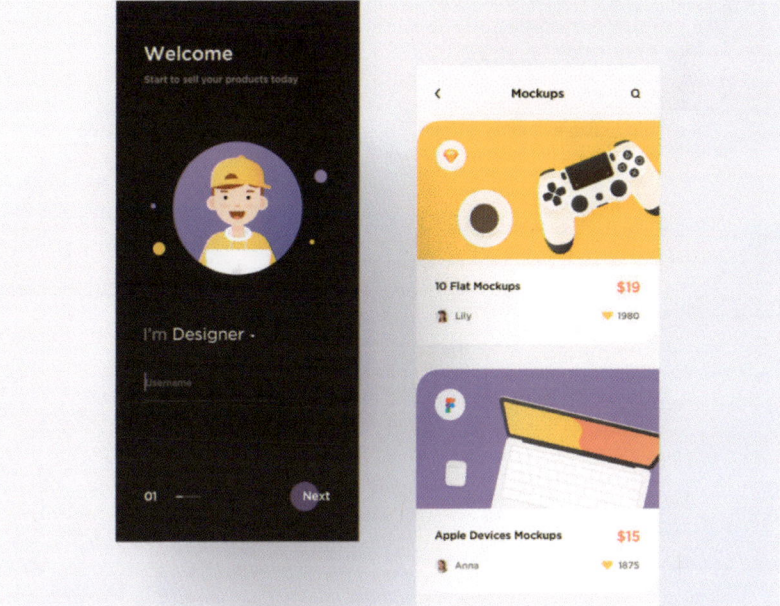

Illustration by  for Fireart Studio

An onboarding process is obligatory for every mobile app today. It is a set of screens displayed to a user during the first interaction with a product. An onboarding tutorial tells users how an app can help them solve their problems, how to use it efficiently, and what are its essential features. A well-set onboarding is the first step to a great user experience.

Digital illustrations can make it even more engaging and easy to understand. Sometimes, several images can explain how to use a product much better than a detailed written tutorial.

Business-Driven Digital Product Design:
Graphic Design In Brand Storytelling

Cute characters on the onboarding screens can assist users in what actions to take to achieve their goals.

Eye-catching illustrations help grow brand recognizability

Digital illustrations, designed according to the brand's identity style, can be used in marketing to grow brand recognizability. Many companies tailor illustrations that follow one style and use them on websites, mobile apps, or marketing visuals. It helps them boost brand awareness and build a strong visual presence online.

An excellent example is a set of humorous illustrations designed by Dmitrij Hladkyi. They depict our team members, besides the number one Fireart Fan. This guy is not our team member, but we like him very much too.

Illustrations by Dmitrij Hladkyi

Business-Driven Digital Product Design:
Graphic Design In Brand Storytelling

To Wrap It Up

Today, more and more brands start realizing that good visual design is as important as engineering. Applying digital illustrations in user interfaces, marketing visuals, and as a part of brand identity, you can make your company memorable to your target audience.

An illustration is a powerful tool for creative story-telling and customer engagement in marketing campaigns. It helps build relationships with users at a more personal level. These are just a few benefits of digital illustration for business.

Business-Driven Digital Product Design:
Graphic Design In Brand Storytelling

5 Ways to Amplify User Interfaces With Digital Illustration

Illustration by Julia Hanke

The functionality is claimed to be the foundation of great UX. However, good design helps users solve their problems, not only by activating product functions but also by triggering positive emotions related to it.

A digital illustration in a user interface design interacts with the user's emotions and provides a better user experience. Here we will outline the top five most effective applications of digital illustration in UI design for web and mobile.

Business-Driven Digital Product Design:
Graphic Design In Brand Storytelling

How To Use Illustrations in User Interface Design?

Welcome users with creative onboarding illustrations

Illustration by Dmitrij Hladkyi

As mentioned, onboarding illustrations are often used to greet users who start interacting with a product. They create the user's first impression of an app and a company, in general.

Using lovely illustrations on the first mobile app screens, you can motivate users to think more positively and increase their loyalty. Imagine a fun character greeting you when you enter an app or website. This cute detail can raise your mood and make your day, doesn't it? Think from the user's perspective. What would you as a user be inspired by? Apply it.

On the other hand, an onboarding illustration is a sign of respect to users. It is a great way to show them that a brand cares about people and wants them to feel comfortable while using a product.

Create the needed associations and mood with interface illustrations

Digital illustration has been one of the most popular UI trends during the last few years, and it is predicted to gain its momentum this year too. It helps set a particular mood and support a specific theme on a website or mobile application. Making the right choice on a color palette, shapes, and visual metaphors, you can build the company associations with trustworthiness, authority, or fun. It helps build a stronger brand image in the users' eyes.

Illustration by Den Klenkov

Moreover, a digital illustration can become a point of the brand's biggest creativity. Use illustrations to express the company's culture and objectives creatively. People will value and remember it.

To reveal the mood-setting power of a digital illustration, let's consider a design created by Andrejs Hairulins for a landing page of the real-estate business software. On the dark-blue background, you can see a milky-white illustration of a big city with skyscrapers and airships in

Business-Driven Digital Product Design:
Graphic Design In Brand Storytelling

the sky. Strict shapes of buildings combined with a minimalist and dark background create the feelings of formality and authority that are often associated with a concept of big business.

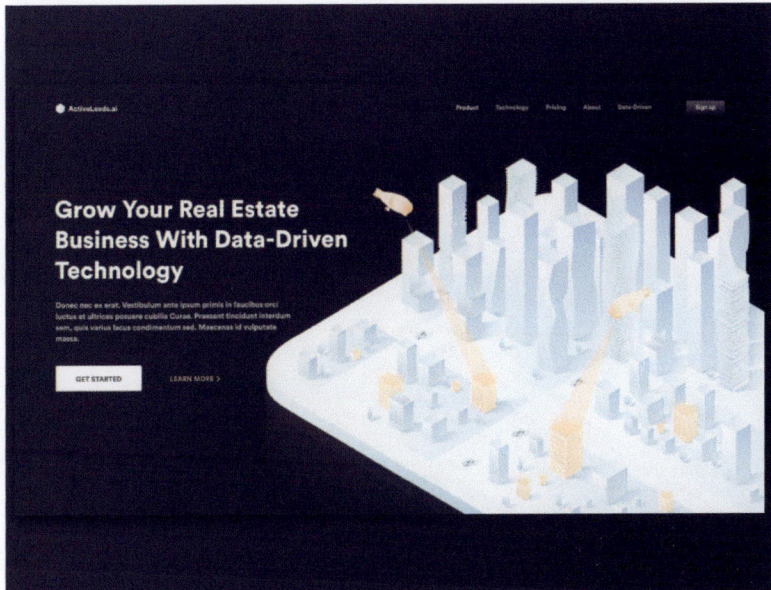

Illustration by Andrejs Hairulins

The airships that are monitoring a city from an aerial view symbolize a data-driven approach to the real-estate business. This mix of shapes, colors, and visual metaphors helps create feelings of trustworthiness and reliability around this brand.

Use illustrations to gamify your UX

Gamification is a powerful tool for user engagement. It is the usage of elements that often appear in games such as medals, stars, badges, stickers, and cups. You can apply them to interfaces to mark the user's progress and reward on a completed action. What can be more enjoyable than to feel yourself a winner? Let users feel it.

A nice example of gamification in UI is a set of funny stickers for a mobile app, created by Fireart designer Hesham Mohamed. These bright characters leave no one indifferent. They work as rewarding elements and make users smile.

Business-Driven Digital Product Design:
Graphic Design In Brand Storytelling

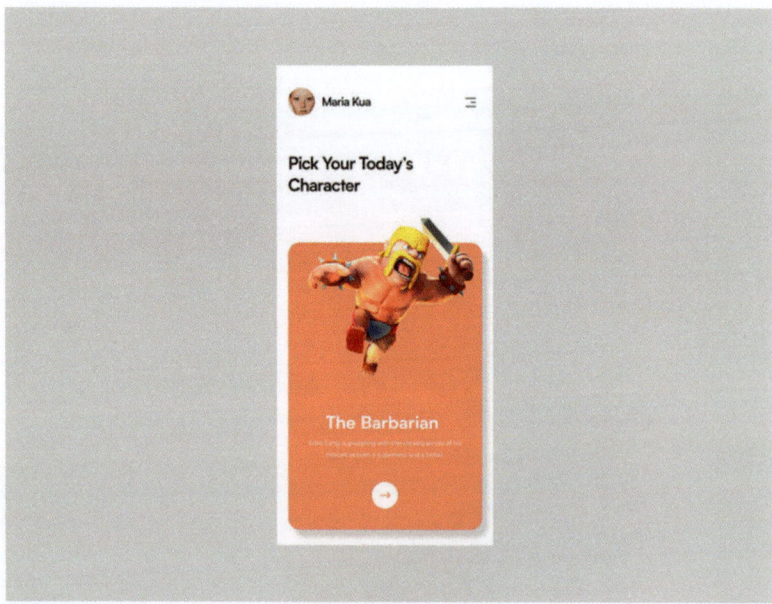

Illustration by Hesham Mohamed

Add personification to a user interface with mascots

Mascots are characters that work as communicators between a brand and users on a website or mobile app. They can shape the bright voice of the user interface and contribute to the company's overall image.

They can even become symbols of a product or the brand's face. The metaphorical nature of these elements breathes life into user interactions. Mascots help create a feeling that the brand communicates with users directly. They are like company representatives that guide users in the online journey.

Illustration by Aslan Almukhambetov

Use tooltips illustrations as the visual prompts

Tooltip illustrations help explain how a product works, encourage users to take specific actions, and clarify app features at different stages of a user journey. They improve user experience and make design friendlier, especially for those users who do not like to read any explanations. Creating a tooltip illustration, a designer should pay attention to details. Each of them shouldn't leave a place for the user's confusion.

This kind of illustration can be a perfect option for tutorials used in mobile apps for kids and teens since a younger user generation does not like to read at all.

Illustration by DAN Gartman

How Digital Illustration Improves UI Design

For the last couple of years, digital illustration has become one of the hottest UI design trends for mobile apps and websites. It helps set a particular mood of a user interface, invokes the needed associations, user emotions, and even conveys the brand's culture.

You can use engaging illustrations to guide users through an app or website, help them interact with a product, and explain its incredible functions. Besides, illustrations can become a part of UI gamification. Badges, stars, stickers, cups, and other rewarding gamifying elements can help engage users even more, give them a visual pleasure, and increase their loyalty.

Useful Reading:

- 7 Tips to Create Engaging Illustrations for Mobile App Onboarding
- 6 Ways Digital Illustration Improves User Experience for Web and Mobile
- The 6 Biggest Illustration Trends That Will Dominate in 2019

Digital Drawing: The How-To Guide on Using Tools for Creativity

Illustration by Lily

"First of all, digital illustration means creativity. There is no assembly instruction manual like for IKEA furniture. Although, there are some practices and hacks on using tools that will help you speed up your workflow."

Dmitrij Hladkyi, Art Director at Fireart Studio

tweet this

Petrol is over and lack of inspiration? Then you are in the right place. Get ready for immersing in our collection of tactics, illustrations, and tips that will help you renew your inner illustrator's power.

Business-Driven Digital Product Design:
Graphic Design In Brand Storytelling

Vector Graphics in Adobe Illustrator

Discover more opportunities of the Pen Tool

Digital drawing with the Pen Tool (P on your keyboard) allows getting acutely precise results that can be particularly useful for tracing photographs or other resources. It requires only a mouse, you mustn't have a drawing tablet. It's the second advantage for designers.

The Pen Tool allows creating a whole variety of lines, curves, and geometric forms - everything can be done with a few masterful mouse clicks. You need only to connect several points called anchors to build lines and paths.

Tip #1. The masterpiece needs your practice. Especially when it comes to dealing with the Pen Tool, which requires you to practice much before you start masterfully applying it. Trace photographs as accurately as you can until you do it like a pro.

Tip #2. Use as a few anchors as possible. Try to space them wisely. Even though a significant number of anchors can make drawing easier, keep in mind that it can also make the eagles bumpier.

Tip #3. Use smart keyboard shortcuts and tools to take more control over your image:
- Shift + C means switching to the Anchor Point tool that allows deleting handles easily.
- Choose the white cursor or A in your keyboard (it enables the Direction Selection Tool) to control handles without anchors.
- To get straight lines, press Shift before creating a new anchor.

Illustration by Magda

Make fun with geometry in a digital illustration

The geometric illustration uncovers the beauty of straight angles, precise radiuses, circles, rectangles, and all other geometric forms possible. It lies in the creative use of the simplest shapes and assembling them into a story on the image.

Dealing with geometry requires you to be exclusively inventive. Think out of the box, cutting, connecting basic geometric shapes, and creating new ones. Everything around us can be broken down into geometry. You can start with your favorite animals - try to depict a dog or cat using circles, squares, rectangles, etc. Experiment. Combine shapes, cut them, reposition, and combine again. Let your creativity fly in the geometry world!

When the image is simplified to the bare geometry, you need to pay particular attention to its perfect composition. To make your geometric illustration sing, you can repeat specific shapes throughout a whole composition. This technique helps create the visual "music" of the image.

Business-Driven Digital Product Design:
Graphic Design In Brand Storytelling

You can add a more pleasant, enjoyable, and friendly look to your illustration by cutting the edges with the Round Corners tool.

Uncover secrets of the hand-drawn illustration

Illustrator is useful not only for building strict shapes but also for a freehand illustration. There are only a few tips on this type of illustration from our team.

The first one: when determining the line's fidelity, you can choose whether to allow an Illustrator to smoothen out your lines or leave them as they are. To set the line's fidelity, click twice on a brush or a pencil icon on the Options panel.

The second tip: you can clean the unnecessary lines applying the Shape Builder Tool, which can be enabled by pressing Shift + M.

Illustration by Magda

Pixel Graphics: Playing With Pixels in Adobe Photoshop

About brushes and textures

Tip #1. Opt for the right brushes and strokes
Actually, this tip is not about brushes. They are surely important but not so crucial as your hard work and excellent composition skills. There are so many useful tools in Photoshop, but we should admit, there are no magic brushes. Like any equipment, no matter how cool and sophisticated it is, it is just a tool that helps implement your creativity.

> "Love blinds us. Don't love anything - an idea, a tool, a graphic, a technique, a technology, a client, or a colleague - too much."
>
> **Adam Judge**, Author of "The Little Black Book of Design"

Tip #2. View a composition from different angles by rotating an image. It helps reveal the slightest composition infelicities and improve the illustration "rhythm." You can apply the Rotate Tool or press R on your keyboard. You can always review back by clicking on the escape key.

Tip #3. Smooth out your strokes with the latest Photoshop update. This new feature is particularly helpful for digital lettering, it allows creating extra-smooth shapes. You can access it on the Options panel.

Tip #4. Avoid heavy brushes. You can download plenty of brushes for Photoshop, however, you should know that some of them can significantly slow down the software and your workflow.

Tip #5. Enjoy the easy switching of a color palette with helpful techniques. You can see how different colors look in your illustration by using two methods in Photoshop. The first one is clicking "lock the transparent pixels" on the Layers panel. It will lock all active pixels in the layer, so when you brush over them, they will change colors without adding new pixels.

Illustrations by Fabin_Raj

Business-Driven Digital Product Design:
Graphic Design In Brand Storytelling

Another method is applying a clipping mask. In this case, you need to create a new layer. Hitting Alt, click on a thin line between two layers. After you do it, you will see a new arrow connecting two layers, a new and previous ones. Now, no matter what colors you choose for the clipping mask, it will appear at a previous layer too.

Tip #6. Experiment with different textures. They can make your 2D image much more "alive" and visually appealing. Just do not overdo using them. The right choice on texture can make your illustration look more "authentic," particularly if you apply scanned real-life visuals. You can create interesting textures on your own, using watercolors, crumpled paper, or ink and import them into Photoshop. To paint your textures, you can use a clipping mask as we have described it earlier.

Illustration by Fabin_Raj

Digitize your sketchbook

Digital drawing doesn't mean that you should abandon real brushes and pens. You can fuse these words by digitizing your sketchbook. If you want to see your hand-drawn artwork in Photoshop, it's better to create a sharp line image and high-contrast shading separately. It allows a computer to read them easily. Then you should just scan a picture or take a high-resolution photo and import it into Photoshop.

Illustration by Dmitrij Hladkyi

When your picture is already here, you should separate it from a white background. To do it, copy a whole image pressing Ctrl/Command + A, open a new channel in the Channels window, and invert it pressing Ctrl/Command + I. To select only your picture, choose "Load channel as selection" at the bottom of the Channels window. Back to the Layer panel and opt here to create a new layer. Then click Ctrl/Command + backspace to paint your selected area.

Voila! Your hand-drawing is digitized. Now you can enhance it, applying the variety of Photoshop tools.

Closing Thoughts

Hey-ho! It has been our guide on how to utilize Illustrator and Photoshop tools more efficiently and create a digital illustration that stands out. We hope you have found inspiration here that will give your illustration work a fresh update and help you look at a blank canvas in a whole new

Business-Driven Digital Product Design:
Graphic Design In Brand Storytelling

light.

Illustration by Dmitrij Hladkyi

Useful Reading:

- CASE STUDY: How to Create The Flat Illustration Design That Stands Out?

Business-Driven Digital Product Design:
Graphic Design In Brand Storytelling

Case Study: How We Created The Collection of Digital Illustrations for Google

"Creativity is inventing, experimenting, taking risks, breaking rules, making mistakes, and having fun."

Mary Lou Cook, Actress

This statement precisely describes our creative process. It is about unexpected experiments, many mistakes combined with inventions, and attempts to give birth to something original and heart-winning. Particularly, when it comes to crafting a digital illustration.

We do not only create pretty pictures. We try to dig into the client's vision, business needs, and draw narrative illustrations that help a brand convey its message and style. Our team believes that a great digital illustration can work as a visual communicator between a brand and its audience.

Here, we are sharing our process and introducing a collection of digital illustrations and user avatars designed for Google Play Games.

When Google Knocked on Our Door

"It's an especially important and memorable case for us since Google has been our first big client. Today, we take pride in presenting in our portfolio many cases related to the world's giant brands, such as Atlassian, Rolls Royce, EY, Huawei, Xiaomi, and plenty of others."

Dima Venglinski, Founder & CEO of Fireart Studio

Task

We have had to create illustrations for the top genres of Google Play Games to make the user experience even more immersive. These images should have reflected the game mood and quickly invoked the user's associations related to a particular genre.

So, we have taken up that challenge and designed illustrations, which are the first thing users see when opening the Google Play Games app along with the gamer's achievement level, top scores, and recent activity.

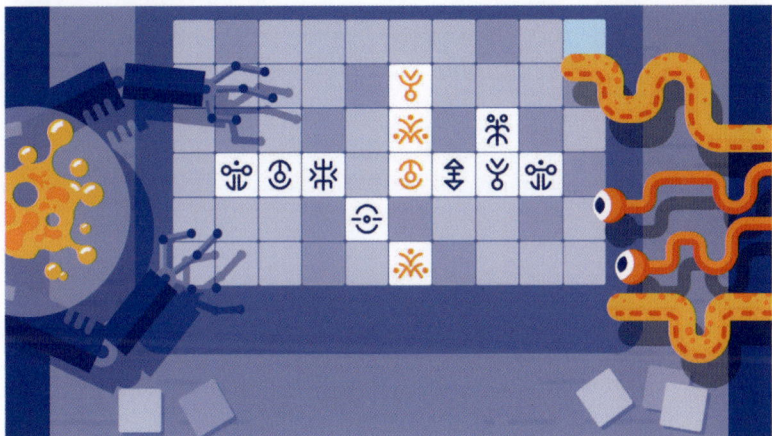

Business-Driven Digital Product Design:
Graphic Design In Brand Storytelling

Solutions

Cover-images for game genres

Our team has designed a collection of illustrations that support different genre themes and let users understand the concept of each game at a glance. We have tried to visualize the movement and activity in narrative scenes.

Character design

We have paid special attention to designing characters. Our illustrators have aimed to make user interactions more "human-like" and strong invoke bright associations with each game. Each character should have conveyed the game idea in a way that corresponds to the mood and voice of a specific genre.

34

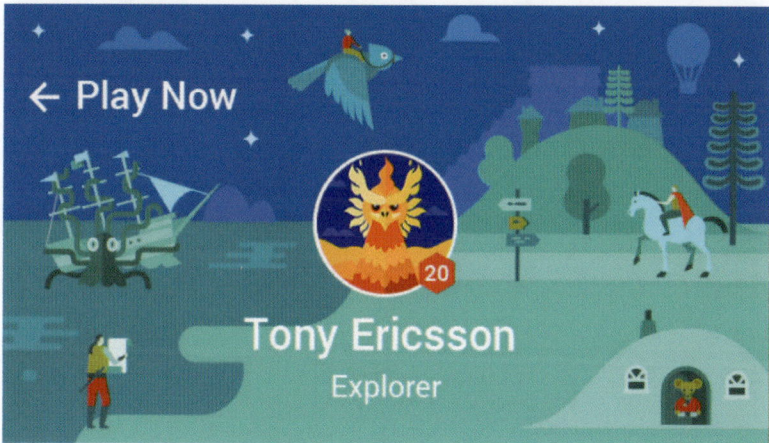

The collection of user avatars
To make Google Plays user experience even more personalized, our graphic design team has created a set of user avatars. The designing distinctive online identities has been an even more significant challenge to us and required a more creative approach.

Business-Driven Digital Product Design:
Graphic Design In Brand Storytelling

We have opted for multi-colored animals, monsters, and aliens. Gamers can notice that these avatars are hints at real human emotions. At the same time, these bright and fun images feel detached from real human identities.

> *"Where do new ideas come from? The answer is simple: differences. Creativity comes from unlikely juxtapositions."*
>
> **Nicholas Negroponte**

Interface design that supports different screen sizes

The design is great only if it looks well on different types of devices. That is why we tried to make all illustrations adjustable to various screen sizes. Here you can see how we have done it.

Business-Driven Digital Product Design:
Graphic Design In Brand Storytelling

Color choices

When deciding on a color palette, we have been inspired by urbanism and the amazing colors of the city jungle. We have noticed the beauty of bold color statements juxtaposed with the muted environments of the contemporary architecture, road signs, pavement marking tape, and sports courts, and applied these incredible color combinations to illustrations for Google Games.

"To communicate with Google's representatives was a real pleasure. The process was amazingly well-organized. We stuck to weekly sprints, often meetings, and quick calls. We did our best to satisfy Google's needs and requirements, but it was not easy.

After that, we got a few other orders from different Google's departments that came to us independently. Departments in such a global enterprise don't communicate with each other much, so they didn't know that we worked with their company before. However, we were happy to know that Google came to us again."

Dima Venglinski, Founder & CEO of Fireart Studio

It was a considerable challenge and a valuable experience for our graphic design team. Would you like to learn more about how we have created digital illustrations for startups and global brands? Visit our website to find **more amazing case studies**.

Chapter II.

Digital Art Goes Live: Explain Business Ideas Creatively With Animation

Illustration by Andy Selimov

Business-Driven Digital Product Design:
Graphic Design In Brand Storytelling

How Can Animation Empower Marketing?

"Animation can explain whatever the mind of man can conceive. This facility makes it the most versatile and explicit means of communication yet devised for quick mass appreciation."

Walt Disney, a pioneer animator and entrepreneur

Animation has evolved brilliantly and become one of the most versatile sales presentation mediums available to a business today. It brings freshness into a marketing strategy and helps build customer loyalty. If used effectively, animation can make a product or service more attractive, sexier, and dynamic-looking. It can uncover a full product's potential displaying its features and advantages creatively.

In this chapter, our motion graphics design team will share insights and ideas on how an animation enables a business to do marketing experiments and find new ways to interact with customers.

Benefits of The Animation for Business

It shows off your brand's personality

Regardless of the industry, customers subconsciously choose a brand that offers something unique. The taste of uniqueness cannot be confused with anything. Both business people and retail customers look for a brand that provides services or products that will help them stand out and innovate as well. The animation is an amazingly effective way to tell about your brand's uniqueness.

Engage your audience. Customers want to communicate and interact with their beloved brands. Start this emotional interaction by grabbing their attention with fun animations on your site or sending holiday emails with the exciting motion graphics. You can also use animated mascots to greet users on onboarding mobile app screens. Everything can be performed in your branding style to emphasize your company's personality.

The animation is easy to understand

"If kids do not understand how to do anything, they would see how somebody is doing it rather than listen to tons of explanations. Visuals are always more powerful and easier to digest. All of us are like kids. We perceive complicated information more easily if it is presented visually and entertains us at the same time."

Dmitrij Hladkyi, Art Director at Fireart Studio

Business-Driven Digital Product Design:
Graphic Design In Brand Storytelling

Sometimes, to explain complex ideas and concepts by using a text copy or flat images is challenging. An animated explainer video is a great solution. A business can communicate sophisticated information to its customers through a short animated story.

Exciting graphics transfers emotions

> "What's most important in animation is the emotions and the ideas being portrayed."
>
> **Ralph Bakshi,** a director of the animated and live-action film

As mentioned above, modern business does not sell products and services but emotions and problem solutions. Or better to say, positive emotions that appear when the customer's problem is solved.

So, anyway, a marketing formula ends in the customer's positive emotions. Animation, in all its beautiful manifestations, is a creative way to interact with your customer emotions. A catchy motion graphics used in the right place and at the right moment can eliminate the negative customer experience, raise the user's mood, and increase loyalty to a brand.

Business-Driven Digital Product Design:
Graphic Design In Brand Storytelling

Animation for Bolt Food by Aslan Almukhambetov for Fireart Studio.
You can watch the full video here

It makes learning entertaining

We learn more quickly when we have fun at the same time. In the highly stressful world, people are overloaded with large volumes of information, so brands need to find new ways to deliver complex ideas in simple forms.

The animation allows to turn learning into entertainment. In the animated video, you can explain any process by breaking it down into short scenes that depict it step by step. You can use a lovely animated mascot to tell about the company's values and business objectives to newcomers. You can also zoom equipment details and educate a worker how to use them to reach a goal.

The animation makes a lasting impression

By using animation in advertising, web design, or mobile apps, brands have a benefit to leaving a memorable impression for their customers. In animated videos, companies can give customers insights into their values and goals, tell about who they are and what they stand for. It significantly increases the chances of building a strong brand recall in the customer's mind.

Business-Driven Digital Product Design:
Graphic Design In Brand Storytelling

Animate your message to promote a new product or service. It will stick out in the customer's memory much longer than text, images, or any other kind of information. Sometimes, even a live-action video is not so exciting and memorable as an animated one.

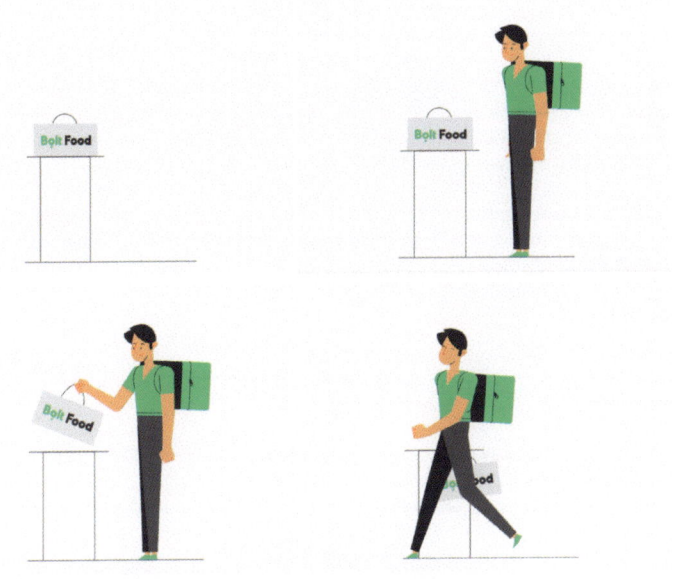

Animation for Bolt Food by Aslan Almukhambetov for Fireart Studio.
You can watch the full video here

It motivates customers to take the preferable actions

According to the latest statistics on video marketing published by Smart Insights, 53% of customers continue engaging with a brand on its website after watching a video on social media. It proves the fact that video content is a powerful tool for customer engagement.

When entering a website for the first time, users would watch a video rather than scroll an entire text copy about the company's products or services. It means that an animated video on a website helps decrease the bounce rate and deliver a message to the audience better.

If users get your message, they are more likely to complete preferred actions, such as filling a contact form or making a purchase. The good idea is to put a call-to-action button at the end of the video so that users can easily switch to a web store or contact form.

Business-Driven Digital Product Design:
Graphic Design In Brand Storytelling

An engaging animation increases customer loyalty

Customer loyalty and trust are often based on brand association. It is what customers think of a company when recalling it, for example, a fun Christmas advertising, a beautiful logotype, overpriced services, or bad customer service.

After a company has improved its customer service or started delivering better quality, customers may still think of a brand from a negative perspective. However, an animated video has the power to change and improve existing brand associations. Furthermore, it can even instill new positive attributes to a brand in the customer's mind.

All in all, people love engaging graphics and video content. If combined with a good sense of humor, peculiarities of the target audience's mentality, and bright design, the animation can raise customer loyalty.

It boosts a website in search rankings

The animation makes us stop scrolling a web page for a while to watch it. In other words, it increases the time spent on your business website. The more time users spend on a particular page, the better it will rank on Google.

Moreover, search engines crawl websites with animation better because they recognize it as valuable content. Google acknowledges that web content is more valuable if users spend more time there than on average. Consequently, it boosts a website in search engines.

The animation is fun and easy to share

We traditionally perceive animated movies as entertainment. The animation feels like a fresh breeze in a marketing strategy. It is a comparatively new approach to promoting products and services. People are more likely to pay attention to animated videos in advertising.

They are engaging, short, and easy-to-understand. These are three essential attributes of a well-performing advert. The more appealing a video is, the more likely it will be fastly spread on the web. People love to share engaging content with their friends, colleagues, and a family on social media, despite it can be even a creative advertising.

Use Motion To Generate The Customer's Positive Emotion

Animation by Dmitrii for Fireart Studio.
You can watch the full video here

Animation provides endless opportunities for creativity and improvisation in marketing. An animated video shouldn't promote products or services directly. Its primary goal is to offer customers the maximum entertainment and make them interested in the brand that delivers it.

Like bees fly where the honey smell is soaring in the air, we are attracted by originality. So, we always spark vivid discussions around brands that shine out on the market with something original. Animation is a powerful tool for engagement that presents the brand's uniqueness.

Useful Reading:

- 5 Reasons Why Animated Explainer Videos Help Promote Your Brand in 2019

Business-Driven Digital Product Design:
Graphic Design In Brand Storytelling

8 Creative Uses of The Animation to Increase CTR and Sales

"If it doesn't sell, it isn't creative."

Debbie Millman, Writer, Designer

Videos are widely recognized as the best way to engage the audience and communicate the brand's message. However, animated videos constitute a particular value for business because they are even more eye-catching and can convey the company's style.

Sometimes, entertainment appears to be even more powerful in marketing than expected. The brand that offers fun to its audience will have a significant advantage among hundreds of its competitors on the market.

Admittedly, we always prefer brands that we love and which we are loyal to. You can start building customer loyalty using animated videos in 8 creative ways, which we are going to explore in this article.

Demonstrate your product features in an engaging way

The power of an animated video is that it turns the impossible into possible, conveying not only the product features but also its mood. At the same time, it can boldly reflect the brand's culture. In an animated video, your imagination can fly high, and there are no limits.

"To infinity...and beyond!"

From the "Toy Story" (1995)

Another advantage of the animation is that you can zoom the smallest details and showcase the internal product components that are invisible in real life.

An excellent example of an animated video that imaginatively shows the product features is "LunarEpic Flyknit," produced by Nike. In the video-promotion of LunarEpic trainers, creators emphasize the product name metaphor and take the viewer to the Moon. Incredible features of the super-comfortable shoes are shown on the background of the breathtaking Moon landscapes.

Business-Driven Digital Product Design:
Graphic Design In Brand Storytelling

Tell about your company's services in explainer videos

Lots of companies in various industries use lovable cartoons to present their services. Business animation has become the top marketing trend today because it helps to stand out.

A great example is an animated video produced by Explain Ninja for Young Alfred, an online marketplace that allows users to compare and buy home insurance more easily. In the one-minute video, the company's services are described in a simple form that seems to be digestible even for a child. This animation is catchy, entertaining, and, most important, it visualizes the brand's voice.

Business-Driven Digital Product Design:
Graphic Design In Brand Storytelling

47

Educate your customers on how to use a particular system or product

The animation is easy to understand, so companies can use it to explain how to use their products or services. It is showcased in the animated <u>video created for Swiss Fin Lab</u>. This animation promotes their ZOA Personal Data Exchange service and demonstrates how to use a system. You can watch the full animated explainer video <u>here</u>.

Business-Driven Digital Product Design:
Graphic Design In Brand Storytelling

Showcase a product or facility that has not yet been built

There is no better way to showcase something that has not yet been built than with the help of 3D-animation. It empowers brands to demonstrate their concepts and ideas which are not implemented yet. Nowadays, companies often use this approach in fundraising campaigns on the platforms, such as Kickstarter and Indiegogo.

The next example of a compelling animated video is a [product trailer for Satechi's Aluminum Keyboard](), featuring various liquid simulations. It is not as colorful as previous examples, but still magnificent and eye-catching. When saying that the animation turns the impossible into possible, we mean visual effects like those presented in this video. They do not display the product's functions but convey its unique style and mood.

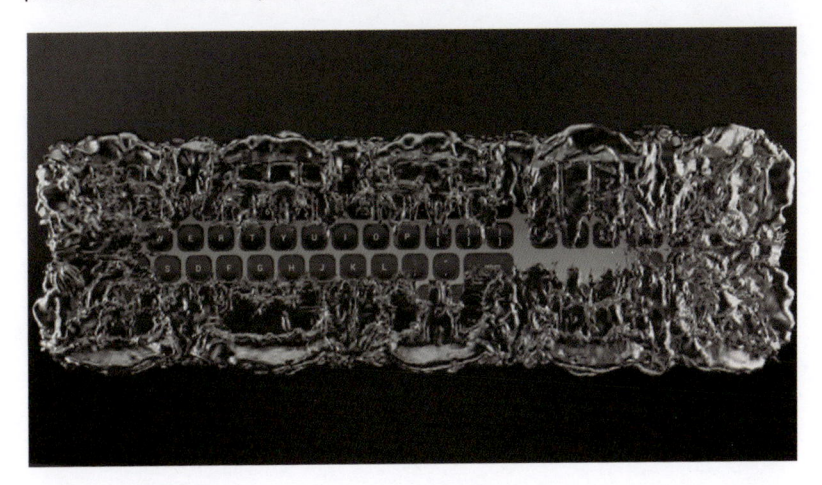

Tell your brand's story

Your product or service may be great, indeed. Despite this, it can face the moment when the number of sales decreases because your competitors take advantage. If your marketing functions like clockwork, but it is focused only on selling products or services, you should switch attention to "selling" your brand's story and building an emotional bond with the audience.

Every brand has something unique. There can be a thousand companies that offer similar products or services, however, each of them has a unique growth story and values. Brands vary like people. All you need is to tell about your brand's peculiarities to your prospective customers.

Business-Driven Digital Product Design:
Graphic Design In Brand Storytelling

The animation is an excellent storytelling tool. It's proved by the experience of big players, like AirBnb, Vans, Lyft, and Chanel.

In the video shared by AirBnb, you can see the full story of its logotype creation. It tells viewers why it looks so, what it symbolizes, and the brand's main values. It doesn't sell AirBnb's services directly, but it sells the brand itself and creates the positive image of the company's image. It's known that a good reputation and authority can sometimes matter much more than the efforts of a whole sales team.

Create a memorable advertising

Your product can look even more enticing if you advertise it in an animated video. In this beautiful video produced for Nespresso, you are quickly immersed in the charming atmosphere of summer. Engaging illustrations are perfectly combined here with memorable summer sounds of pouring drinks, clinking ice cubes, gently lapping waves, rustling bushes, birds, and chirping crickets.

This advert looks memorable and creates a lasting impression. After you have watched it, you still are thinking of summer and, maybe… about that alluring summer drink promoted there too.

Boost your social media content

90% of successive social media marketing lies in eye-catching visual content. Short animations are widely used today as the best tool for audience engagement on social media.

A great example is a short animation that promotes the opening of Nhinjo Sushi & Grill Restaurant. In this case, 20 seconds of a lovely animated video seem to be enough to tell all the important information about the restaurant and the upcoming event. People are more likely to pay attention to such content on social media than any other.

Boost email marketing effectiveness by using animation

You can entertain your customers by sending them animated offers via email. For example, the top sportswear giant Nike sends its customers Birthday greetings with the catchy animation. The illustrations below demonstrate an animated banner created by Nike last year.

To Wrap It Up

The animated video has become one of the most popular ways to attract the target audience and increase sales. It can be used to tell your brand's story, demonstrate product features, describe services, boost social media marketing, email campaigns, and much more.

Business-Driven Digital Product Design:
Graphic Design In Brand Storytelling

Hopefully, after reading this small collection of our team's ideas on how to use animation, you will be inspired enough to rethink your marketing strategy and consider animation as its valuable constituent.

Useful Reading:

- The Power of Motion Graphics in App Development
- 3 Smart Ways To Engage Users With Animation
- How to Delight Users With Animation

Lifting The Veil To Our Animation Production Process

The animation production pipeline is a journey of the movie from the creator's brain to the screen for the world to see. During this complex process, we make flat illustrations alive.

When producing animations for our clients, we often hear questions like "Why does this simple character take so much time to be animated?" or "why can't we just change the camera angle on this shot?" Here we will answer them and share our team's insights on the magic of animation, which can be useful for both business owners and motion designers.

Stages of The Animation Production Process

Scriptwriting

Every cool movie begins with a great script. It is a fundamental element of a killer explainer video. Before designing illustrations, we discuss the animation concept with a client and in-team. The script is the essence of the movie and the reference point for all the other elements involved in the production process.

"Conceptualization is the initial stage of any design process. At this step, we don't think of what we should show to the target audience but what we should say to them. The scriptwriting is a process of creating a story that can successfully deliver the brand's message to its customers. And we should think of how to make this message as clear and memorable as possible."

Dmitrij Hladkyi, Art Director at Fireart Studio

Storyboarding

After the script is nailed, we create several storyboards and discuss them with our client. A storyboard demonstrates how a script will play out on the screen scene by scene.

> "At this step, we think of what we should show to the audience. It is basically a very rough comic book that displays all our ideas of visuals and directing stuff, like camera angles, transitions, etc."
>
> **Valeria Rimkevich**, Art Director at Fireart Studio

Illustrations

When the storyboard is finalized, we move forward to crafting illustrations. We think of colors, shapes, and the overall style of the future video. At this stage, the client can see full-color visuals that give an accurate idea of how the video will look like. We start nailing a motion design only after we have agreed on all sketches with the client.

The production time and budget mostly depend on the complexity of illustrations. For instance, this illustration needs less time to be created since it has comparatively simple shapes and colors.

Business-Driven Digital Product Design:
Graphic Design In Brand Storytelling

On the contrary, the next illustration is much more complicated because it displays a whole variety of tones, sophisticated shapes, and textures. Consequently, it needs more time to be produced.

Illustration by [Dmitrij Hladkyi](#)

Animation

It is when all the motion design magic happens. At this stage, we breathe life into images and make them running, jumping, smiling, talking, and doing everything that is needed to convey the marketing message creatively. Further, we will describe the animation process in detail.

Sound Design

Illustration by SEM JI

When the design is animated, it's time to put an engaging sound over it. Cooperating with talented voice actors, we create a sound plan that reinforces a message of the explainer video. We choose an accent that will be easily understood by the target audience and set the right pace of the sound. We also add background music and other sounds to make the video even more lovable.

Hints for Creating Three Types of Animation

In the explainer video production process, we usually use three animation types: keyframes, frame-by-frame, and 3D. The budget and time of the animation production much depend on the type of animation the client prefers.

Business-Driven Digital Product Design:
Graphic Design In Brand Storytelling

Keyframing

The keyframing is an animation technique which is the most widely used by motion designers nowadays. It defines the starting and ending points of any smooth transition. The main idea lies in the process of keyframe manipulating, which happens when you place a circle on the point A, anchor the frame here, then establish the motion time, putting a circle to the point B and setting another frame here.

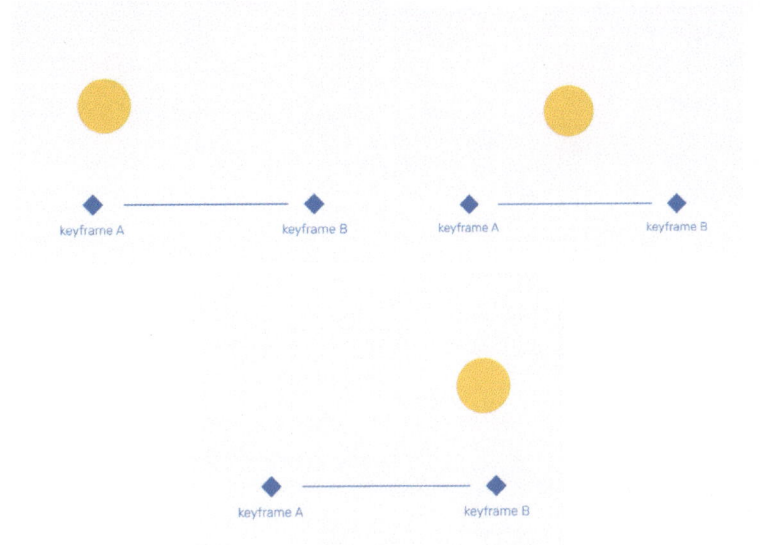

keyframe A   keyframe B   keyframe A   keyframe B

keyframe A   keyframe B

Keyframing makes the objects move. It's been the first way to make animation magic. You can see it implemented in this explainer video produced for LaunchCloud by our motion designers.

However, this type of animation has its limitations. For instance, all the objects that are moving in the illustrations are flat.

Below, you can see an illustration created for an animated video created for Plato. The next picture shows how the same scene looks in the three-dimensional space. It means that, unfortunately, we cannot change the camera position to show the same scene from a different angle. Actually, we can, but it needs us to create a new set of illustrations that display the scene from that angle.

Business-Driven Digital Product Design:
Graphic Design In Brand Storytelling

Illustration from our Plato App

Another limitation of the keyframing technique is that it is difficult to animate the objects, like human hands, by using only keyframes. In the video, hands usually perform a whole variety of actions. They change positions, rotate, and imitate other real-life micro-movements. The

Business-Driven Digital Product Design:
Graphic Design In Brand Storytelling

keyframing does not allow to achieve all the desirable visual effects. But, we can do it by creating the frame by frame.

The frame-by-frame animation

Frame-by-frame animation is the oldest and the most traditional type. Even our ancestors have used it to create the first cartoons. It means drawing every single frame manually.

Although this animation type may seem out-of-date, it still is very popular today. It allows animating almost all the objects possible. The sky's the limit. Or the abilities of the animator's imagination.

When applying a frame-by-frame technique, you do not need to think of technical difficulties related to keyframes and rigging. The objects will look more alive and natural, although this process is more time-consuming and requires more designers to work on it, which means the higher cost of production.

Since not every business has the animation budget like the good old Disney, many motion designers commonly suggest clients to animate every second frame (not every single). It allows reducing the price because the designer should create only 12 frames instead of 24 frames for each second of animation. It doesn't affect the animation quality, the change is almost invisible

Business-Driven Digital Product Design:
Graphic Design In Brand Storytelling

to the human eyes. This trick may save up to 50% of the video-production time and is frequently used by motion design studios all over the globe.

Here are a few examples of explainer videos that we produced by using frame-by-frame animation for our clients Pipedrive and Swiss Fin Lab.

3D Animation

Usually, we apply 3D animation to do sophisticated object rotations and change the angle of view. Imagine that you need to render and animate a fast-rotating car for an explainer video. It will be much easier and faster to do it in 3D than drawing it frame-by-frame or by using keyframes.

The 3D animation process includes modeling, texturing, and lighting. At the initial stage, we create an object. After, we apply different colors and textures. At the last step, we add lights and shadows.

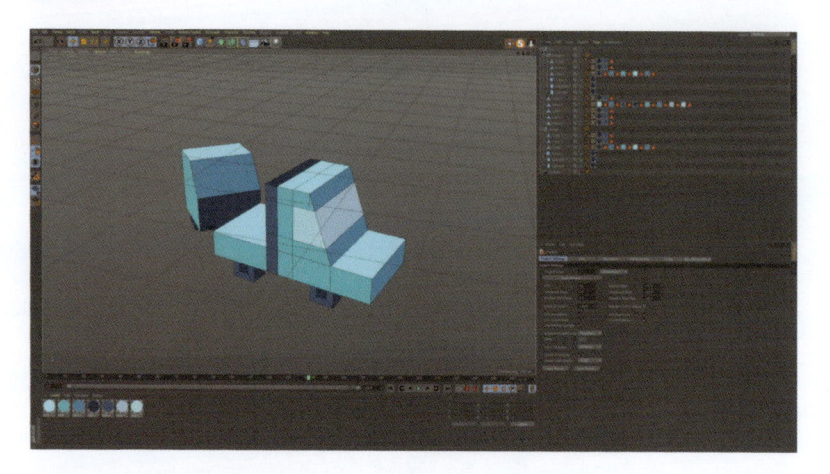

The great sample of 3D animation is a video created for Boostation.

Furthermore, we can apply 3D to animate separate elements. For example, the video is created in 2D, but there are a few fast-rotating objects which can be animated only in the 3D space. This type of animation opens many opportunities for creativity, but it needs a designer to have substantial technical knowledge.

Business-Driven Digital Product Design:
Graphic Design In Brand Storytelling

The Magic of The Character Animation

"Believe in your character. Animate with sincerity."
Glen Keane, Animator, Illustrator, Author

The character takes the additional time to be animated. Here we will consider three main types of characters and production stages.

Production Stages

Character design

We draw a silhouette, think of the character's mood, and select a color palette. We also prepare a character for rigging. It means that the character should be drawn in various body positions and wearing different clothes since they may change during the video. For example, if the character usually wears a hat, we should draw the head without a hat too because the story may dictate a hat to fall down.

Rigging

During the rigging, we get a character ready for the animator's manipulations. By setting controllers and deformers, we can make a character move like a puppet.

Animation

We add motion and make everything "alive." To animate characters, we usually use keyframing and frame-by-frame techniques.

Types of Animated Characters

We used to divide the characters by their complexity.

Simple

A "simple" character is drawn and animated in only one position. It doesn't turn the head, and neither changes a position nor a facial expression. For example, such a character can sit behind a laptop and type something without doing any sudden movements and rotations. It is a simple animation that doesn't require much time to be produced.

Complex

A simple animation can display movements, like running from one side to another. In case if a character is walking, then stops to check a phone (for example), and continues walking again, this scene is defined as a complex animation. It requires more time for rigging and creating complex body mechanics that is more time-consuming.

Advanced

This character usually looks more engaging and naturally. It runs, then stops to check a phone, turns around, and, understanding that he or she still doesn't know where to go, starts crying and continues walking, being in a low-spirited body position. This type of character is called "advanced" since it needs much more effort to be animated.

Closing Thoughts

The animation production process is incredibly exciting and sophisticated at the same time. To produce a catchy and heart-taking animation, a motion designer needs to utilize the full creative potential and strategic-thinking.

We have been happy to share our vision and experience with you. Hopefully, our insights will help turn the animation into a headache-free process and understand what influences the animation cost and quality.

Useful Reading:

- Animation For Marketing
- The Ultimate Animation Guide by Fireart Studio. This Will Help You Understand Our Process Better

Case Study: How We Produced an Explainer Video for Swiss Fin Lab

During the last seven years at Fireart Studio, we have perfected the process of designing, building, scripting, and editing explainer videos for business. Today, we would like to share a valuable experience we have got by producing an animated video for Swiss Fin Lab, a fintech development company.

Task

We got a task to create an explainer video that should have given the lowdown on ZOA, the personal data exchange solution developed by Swiss Fin Lab. The video was expected to be a quick and easy-to-understand explanation of this service. It had to guide customers on how to use a ZOA system and tell about its benefits.

Business-Driven Digital Product Design:
Graphic Design In Brand Storytelling

What Is ZOA?

ZOA allows users to manage their personal data stored at different organizations more easily. Its distinctive feature is the easy-to-use questionnaire workflow that helps take control over your data inventory and data processing software across all legal entities.

Combining concise language and appealing illustrations, we produced the video that was aimed to improve communication between Swiss Fin Lab and its customers. Here is how.

The Explainer Video Production Process

To create an animation that meets the client's needs and business objectives, our team passed on the following stages:

Initial research

At that stage, we conducted detailed audience and market research to have a better understanding of people we were crafting video content for.

A pre-production stage

It included scriptwriting and storyboarding. At the early pre-production stage, our designers created a set of sketches that displayed the basic concepts of the future explainer video. Each picture in a storyboard had to support the brand's style, reflect the company's mission, and meet

Business-Driven Digital Product Design:
Graphic Design In Brand Storytelling

business goals. Every sketch and character was discussed with the Swiss Fin Lab representatives. After we agreed on the stylistic preferences and the main message of the video, our team moved forward to the production stage.

Business-Driven Digital Product Design:
Graphic Design In Brand Storytelling

Production

Fireart illustrators created all the needed graphics following the algorithm mentioned above. They opted for a color palette and style that corresponded to the brand identity design.

We faced a few challenges on the way. When crafting a scene with a rotating calendar, we had to use 3D animation since the object was too complicated to be performed by manipulating the keyframes. Moreover, while producing a shot with a rotating rough hand holding a hammer, we

Business-Driven Digital Product Design:
Graphic Design In Brand Storytelling

had to combine a few approaches. The hand was animated by using a traditional frame-by-frame technique, and a hammer was rendered separately in the 3D space.

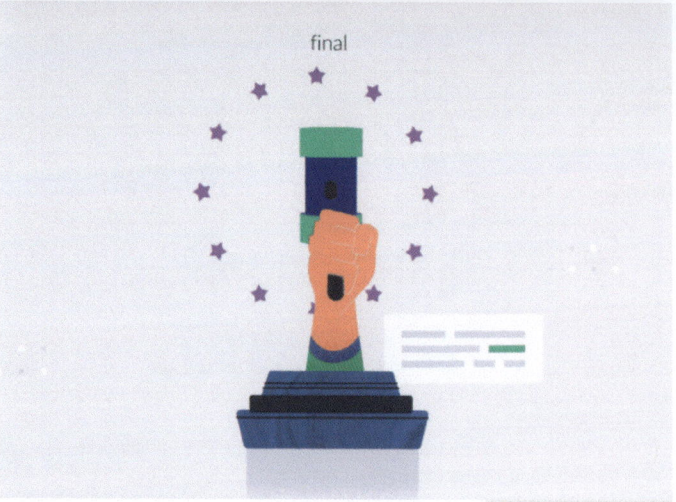

Business-Driven Digital Product Design:
Graphic Design In Brand Storytelling

Besides that, animating a human hand itself appeared to be a considerable challenge for us. Due to the complexity of the hand movements, it was possible to animate them only in After Effects. Later, a frame-by-frame sequence of the hand animation was parented to the character's elbow.

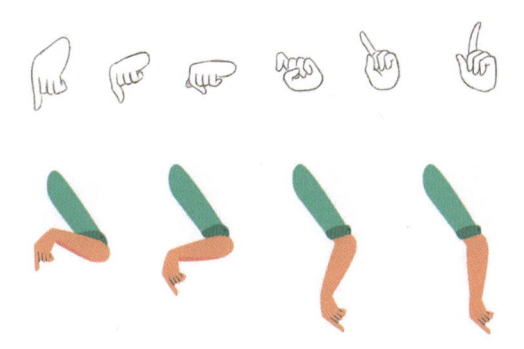

All the scenes represented in the digital illustrations were assembled into the animated story that was aimed to convey the concepts of a ZOA service, assist users, and constitute an emotional and aesthetic appeal to customers.

Post-production

At that stage, we edited the video and enhanced visual effects. After the sound and the visual part were combined, an explainer video was ready. You can watch the finalized version of the video for Swiss Fin Lab here.

Final Thoughts

To create a video that meets the client's needs, brings visual pleasure, and satisfies business goals is not an easy task to do. Despite explainer videos are usually short and look simple, they require much effort and skills to be produced, as it is displayed in the creative process we have shared above.

We hope that our expertise will help you create an animated video that brings success to the business. Undoubtedly, a colossal motion design experience is advantageous in the video production process; however, thinking out of the box may appear to be even more critical. Our team wishes you not to be afraid of doing new experiments since only creativity makes a brand unique for its customers and distinguishes it among others.

Business-Driven Digital Product Design:
Graphic Design In Brand Storytelling

Conclusion

Modern businesses are expected to be creative, innovative, and ever-evolving in everything they do, especially when it comes to marketing, branding, and visual online presence.

Many brands use stock images and videos in their marketing. However, those businesses that use custom digital illustrations and animated videos can offer their audience uniqueness, originality, and entertainment. These are essential factors of effective marketing. All of them can be achieved if to apply the power of graphic design to your brand's image.

In this book, Fireart illustrators and motion designers have shared with you their valuable tips and practices on how to create pictures and videos that make a company shine on the Internet. We have been happy to introduce this collection of our thoughts, graphic design use cases, hacks, and examples.

The markets are full of alternatives to products and services across various industries. However, keep in mind that each brand is unique. You should just know how to uncover this uniqueness to your audience. Graphic design can help you do it.

Stand up and stand out! We hope that this book has inspired you to take up new exciting design challenges and do creative experiments that will help your business grow.

Let's keep in touch and meet again in our next book!

Yours,
Fireart Team

Business-Driven Digital Product Design:
Graphic Design In Brand Storytelling

Feel free to share this eBook with your friends and colleagues!

Stay updated with the latest news and insights from our team by following **Fireart Blog**.

Do you have a question or an idea to discuss? Don't hesitate to drop us a note!

Email: client@fireart.studio

Find us on social networks

fireart.studio

Business-Driven Digital Product Design:
Graphic Design In Brand Storytelling

Printed in Great Britain
by Amazon